# Control Freak

## HORMONES, THE BRAIN, AND THE NERVOUS SYSTEM

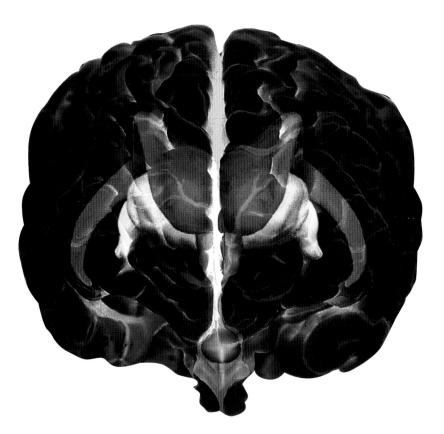

Steve Parker

Chicago, Illinois

For information, address the publisher
Raintree, 100 N. LaSalle, Suite 1200
Chicago, IL 60602
Customer Service   888-363-4266
Visit our website at www.raintreelibrary.com

Printed and bound in China, by South China Printing
Company Ltd

10 09 08 07 06
10 9 8 7 6 5 4 3 2 1

**Library of Congress Cataloging-in-Publication Data**
Parker, Steve.
    Control freak! / Steve Parker.
      p. cm. -- (Body talk)
    Includes index.
    ISBN 1-4109-1875-0 (lib. bdg.) -- ISBN 1-4109-1882-3
(pbk)
    1. Neurophysiology--Juvenile literature.  2. Nervous
system--Juvenile literature.    I. Title.  II. Series: Parker,
Steve. Body talk.
  QP361.5.P372 2006
  612.8--dc22
                                                2005022269

**Acknowledgments**
The publishers would like to thank the following for
permission to reproduce photographs:
Action Plus p. 40 (Glyn Kirk), p. 6 (Mike Hewitt), p. 8
(Neil Tingle); Alamy pp. 36-37, 21 (Kolvenbach), p. 19
(Profimedia. CZ s.r.o.); Corbis pp. 6-7, 18-19, 34-35; 20
(Bob Gelberge), pp. 4-5 (George Hall), pp. 16-17 (Lawrence
Manning), p. 29 (Michael Kevin Daly), p. 22 (Rolf
Bruderer), p. 27 (Varie/Alt), p. 35 (Creatas); Getty Images
pp. 20-21; 10 (Joe McNally), pp. 28-29 (Image Bank), pp.
12, 37 PhotoDisc), pp. 5, 5, 24-25, 33, 40-41 (Stone),p. 43
(Taxi); Harcourt Education/Tudor Photography pp. 15, 30-
31; Science Photo Library pp. 42; 10-11, 22-23 (AJ Photo),
p. 14 (CNRI), pp. 26-27 (Dr M.A. Ansary), pp. 23, 39
(James Holmes), p. 39 (Michael Donne),p.  9 (Pasieka), pp.
32-33 (TEK Image), p. 38 (Zephyr), pp. 12-13
(Superstock).
Cover photograph of head with wires reproduced with
permission of Tips.
Artwork by Darren Lingard and Jeff Edwards.

Every effort has been made to contact copyright holders of
any material reproduced in this book. Any omissions will
be rectified in subsequent printings if notice is given to the
publishers.

The paper used to print this book comes from sustainable
resources.

**Disclaimer**
All the Internet addresses (URLs) given in this book were
valid at the time of going to press. However, due to the
dynamic nature of the Internet, some addresses may have
changed, or sites may have ceased to exist since publication.
While the author and publishers regret any inconvenience
this may cause readers, no responsibility for any such
changes can be accepted by either the author or the
publishers.

Dedicated to the memory of Lucy Owen

# Contents

Any words appearing in the text in bold, **like this**, are explained in the glossary. You can also look out for them in "Body language" at the bottom of each page.

# Total Control

You are blasting through the sky in a supersonic jet plane, traveling at incredible speed, the length of three soccer fields every second!

You need total concentration and razor-sharp **senses**. Your eyes dart about the dials and controls, checking engine power and fuel levels. Your hands feel the control stick and your body detects the plane's every twist and turn.

Through the headset, your ears monitor messages from your commander back at base. Your mouth is dry and you feel the buzz of **epinephrine** as your heart thumps and your muscles tense.

## Body machine checklist

✔ **Sensors** – eyes, ears, nose, tongue, skin

✔ Hard drive and central processor – the brain

✔ Download – **nerves** carry signals from sensors to brain

✔ Upload – nerves take signals from brain to muscles

✔ Life long guarantee – substances called **hormones** control growth and inner body processes

With the roar of the ➤ jets, the pilot's senses are highly alert and his brain is in complete command.

**Body language**   epinephrine hormone that gets the body ready for quick action if needed. It is produced during exercise and when the body experiences fear and excitement.

## The brain

All this information from your senses feeds into the main control center, your brain. Every second, you analyze your speed, height, and direction. You are so highly trained that you hardly have to think about some of this. Your brain seems to have its own automatic pilot. In fact, your brain has to control one amazing and complex machine—your body—so that your body can control another incredible and complicated machine, the plane.

As you fly such a fast, powerful, and dangerous jet with supreme skill, you really need to be a control freak!

## Find out later

*What is your brain doing while you are asleep?*

*Why do children and adults like different flavors?*

*What happens when you are scared?*

**hormones** chemical substances made by glands that help the body carry out various processes

5

# Control Center

If you could see your brain, you might not be impressed. It is a dome-shaped lump that looks like pinkish-grey jelly, and weighs about 3 pounds (1 1/2 kilograms). It has deep grooves and wrinkles over its surface, and a stalk at the base.

But your brain is the most exciting place you can imagine. It is where you think, have ideas, store memories, decide to take actions, control movements, work out problems, daydream, worry, and have feelings like sadness, excitement, and joy. It is the place where your personality comes alive. In many ways, your brain is YOU.

## Use it, don't lose it

The soft, delicate brain is well shielded by the hard **skull** bone around it. But sometimes the brain needs extra protection, like a helmet or hardhat. It is important to wear good protection whenever you take part in activities like rock climbing or cycling. In extreme sports such as skeleton sledding (right), a helmet is essential!

Medical scanner machines ➤ show a living, working brain. Around it are thin cushionlike layers called **meninges,** that help protect it.

**glucose** sugar obtained from the breakdown of carbohydates in food. It is the body's main source of energy.

## Big or small?

Like other body parts, brains vary in size and shape from person to person. But there is no link between brain size and intelligence. Otherwise, some creatures would be much smarter than us. The sperm whale has the world's biggest brain, about 18 pounds (8 kilograms). But as far as we know, it is not a genius! It is what you do with your brain, rather than its size, that is important.

The more you use your brain by thinking and remembering, the faster and more accurate you will become at these processes. Just as physical exercise can increase your muscle power, mental exercise like learning and solving problems can increase your brain power.

brain          meninges

## Thinking uses lots of energy!

Your brain makes up 2 percent of your body weight. Yet it needs 20 percent of your body's energy. For its size, the brain uses ten times more energy than other body parts. The energy comes from food and goes to the brain in the form of a sugar called **glucose**.

### DID YOU KNOW?

Overall, the body is about 65 percent water. But the brain is even more watery – about 75 percent. If you could squish a brain like a sponge, you would squeeze out enough water to fill a one quart (one liter) juice carton.

**meninges**   three thin layers around the brain and spinal cord that protect and nourish them. They are called the dura mater, arachnoid, and pia mater.
**skull**   main bone in the head, which is really more than 20 bones joined together

## Super skills

When you learn skillful movements, you are using your **cerebellum.** This is the rounded, wrinkled part at the back area of the brain. It makes your muscles move with split-second control.

## Where did you get that idea?

Your brain has several main parts, each doing different jobs, but all joined so they work together. The biggest part is the large wrinkled dome on top, the **cerebrum.** It makes up more than three-quarters of the whole brain. This is where you have most of your thoughts and ideas, and where you understand information from your eyes, ears, and other **sense organs.**

▼ The brain is very complicated, with many parts doing different jobs, but they all work together smoothly.

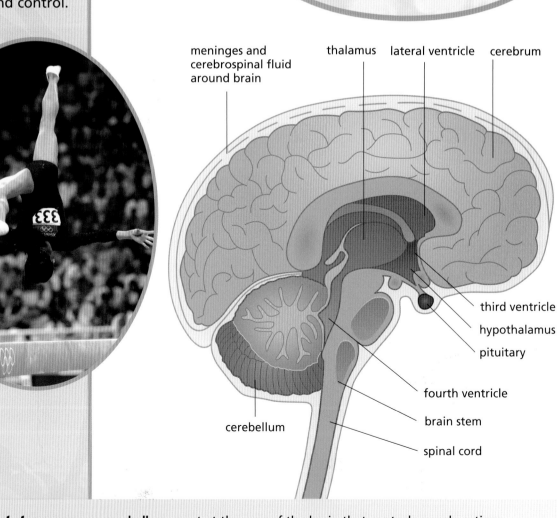

meninges and cerebrospinal fluid around brain

thalamus   lateral ventricle   cerebrum

third ventricle

hypothalamus

pituitary

fourth ventricle

brain stem

spinal cord

cerebellum

cerebellum   part at the rear of the brain that controls muscle actions

## Inner parts

Are you feeling wide awake or tired and sleepy? In the middle of the brain is a part shaped like two eggs, the **thalamus.** This helps to control your awareness, from being fully alert to daydreaming, feeling tired or sleeping soundly. It also helps to pass information coming in from the senses to the huge cerebrum above.

## Small but important

When did you last feel really hungry, very thirsty, or have strong emotions like anger or great joy? All these feelings are based in a part just below the thalamus, called the **hypothalamus.** It is only as big as a grape, but it has huge effects on the way you behave.

## Hollow heads

Did you know that your brain is hollow? Inside it are four small chambers, called **ventricles,** filled with a pale yellow liquid, **CSF,** or the **cerebrospinal fluid.** CSF covers the outside of the brain, too. As it slowly flows, it brings nourishment to the brain and takes away waste. Of course, like other body parts, the brain also has a blood supply to bring nourishment and remove wastes.

## Brain bricks

All body parts are made of microscopic building blocks called **cells.** The brain's cells are called **nerve cells.** Each has long arms that almost touch those of other nerve cells (below). They pass on tiny electrical signals called nerve messages. This scan shows nerve cell fibers.

### TOO MANY TO IMAGINE

- There are more than 100,000,000,000 nerve cells in the brain – that's 100 billion.

- Each is linked to thousands of others, so the connections between all the nerve cells number trillions of trillions.

- Every day up to 10,000 brain cells die. But that's normal. There are so many cells left.

**cerebrum**   large upper portion of the brain with white matter inside and a surface layer of gray matter. It receives information from the senses.

## No-pain brain!

The brain has no touch or pain **sensors,** so cannot feel anything, not even the knife of a brain surgeon. Amazingly, people can be wide awake during a brain operation (below). However, parts around the brain do have pain sensors, so an injection is given to numb the area.

## Think!

Every time you look, listen, feel, read, write, and move, you use your **cerebral cortex.** This is the name for the thin covering of the brain's main part, the **cerebrum.** Spread out, the cortex would be about as large as a pillowcase and almost as thin. But it has lots of deep folds and wrinkles so it fits inside your **skull.** Each area of the cortex has a special task, as you will see later.

▼ Nerve messages pass around the brain as tiny electrical signals. Sensor pads on the skin detect these faint signals, and show them as wavy or spiky lines called an **EEG (electroencephalogram).**

**axons**　parts of a nerve cell that take messages from the main cell body to other nerve cells

**dendrites**　parts of a nerve cell that take messages from nerve cells to the main cell body

## Gray and white

The cortex is the main place for our thoughts, decisions, and awareness. This is what we call our mind.

The cortex is made of billions of **nerve cells** linked together by their spiderlike arms, or **dendrites.** Every second these carry millions of messages. The cortex is colored gray and is sometimes called gray matter.

Underneath the cortex is white matter, which makes up most of the inside of the cerebrum. This contains long wirelike parts from nerve cells, known as nerve fibers or **axons.** The fibers link the nerve cells of the cortex to other parts of your brain.

### Left or right?

The main brain has two halves, called **cerebral hemispheres.** These look similar but work differently. The left side deals with words, numbers, scientific skills, and working through problems. The right side deals with shapes, colors, sounds, music, imagination, and ideas. Which one do you use most?

"It was the darkest, blackest night I could remember. Far away, an owl hooted. A car roared past, and I smelled its exhaust fumes. Suddenly, a huge flash of lightning lit up the street, and a giant clap of thunder shook the earth ..."

**Can you see, hear, smell and feel this story? You only need the words. Then your mind, imagination and memory take over.**

**sensor** part which detects something, like light, sound, or the amount of a chemical and sends messages to the brain

## What are memories made of?

Can you remember a recent happy time like your birthday, a holiday, or a fun day playing? Take a short time to bring back those memories. Are they just sights or scenes? Or can you also remember sounds, smells, and perhaps your feelings, too?

The more you think back, the more you can remember. Memories are more complicated than they seem.

## The nerve message pathways

But what are memories? Your brain has billions of **nerve cells** linked together in trillions of ways to carry nerve messages. A memory is probably a set of links that carry a nerve message along a certain path.

Our strongest memories are ➤ usually exciting or strange events that were very good, very bad, or very scary.

## Brain drain

The brain keeps short-term memories for just a few minutes or hours. These are usually less important, like what we ate for lunch. Soon we forget them. Otherwise, the brain would be full of unimportant information.

Each time you recall a memory, the nerve message goes along its path from one nerve cell to the next, and the links stay fresh.

So using a memory often keeps the paths open and the links strong. Memories that aren't used much fade away, the links are lost, and you forget.

## Memory centers

Memories are stored in several parts of the brain. These include the main **cortex** over the top and also parts inside like the **hippocampus.** How would you remember a word like hippocampus? Would there be strange pictures on this memory's pathway, like a hippo in a tent?

### I remember, years ago ...

The brain stores long-term memories for almost a lifetime. They include very important information like our names, where we live, family and friends, birthdays, holidays, and perhaps sad events like the death of a much-loved pet.

### QUIZ

Look at these pictures for 20 seconds. Then close the book and try to draw them. Which is easiest to copy? Probably the right-hand one.

Both pictures have the same parts. But the right one has a familiar pattern that means something, making it easier to remember.

# The Body's Intranet

The Internet is made up of the links between millions of computers all around the world. Countless messages pass around this network every second. The body has lots of information passing around inside it, too.

The brain receives and sends out messages all the time to control body parts and make sure they work together. This information is in the form of tiny electrical signals called impulses. They pass along wirelike parts called **nerves** that link the brain to all body parts. This system of nerves is like the body's own inner network, or intranet.

## What a nerve!

Your main nerve is the **spinal cord,** carrying information between your brain and your body. It runs from the base of your brain, down inside the bones of your neck and back. All the way down, 31 pairs of nerves branch off to your various body parts.

base of brain

skin on back of neck

brain

spinal cord

radial nerve

sciatic nerve

tibial nerve

windpipe    back bones    spinal cord

The body's nerves go from the ▲ brain and its main nerve, the spinal cord, to every part. The nerves branch smaller and smaller, right into the fingertips and ends of the toes.

**nerves**   stringlike tissue that carries messages around the body as tiny pulses of electricity

## Coming and going

Nerves look like pieces of shiny, elastic, gray string. Inside each nerve is a bundle of **nerve fibers**, much thinner than hairs. These are the long, wirelike parts of **nerve cells** that carry nerve messages.

Your brain knows what the messages mean because of where they come from. For example, messages from tiny touch **sensors** in your hand tell you that you are holding this book.

### GET ON YOUR NERVES

- If all the nerves in your body could be joined end to end, they'd stretch about 47 miles (76 kilometers).
- Your thickest nerve is your **sciatic nerve**, in your upper leg, which is about as wide as your thumb.
- Your spinal cord is about as thick as your little finger.
- One of the shortest main nerves, only the length of your thumb, is from your eye to your brain.

## Pins and needles

If you sit or lie awkwardly for a while, you may feel a horrible tingling or buzzing, sometimes known as pins and needles. This may happen because a nerve is squashed. As soon as you rub and stretch, the nerve gets back to normal and the tingling feeling goes away.

**sciatic nerve**   nerve that runs from the pelvis down the back of each leg to the foot

## Info in and out

Every second, your brain receives and sends millions of messages along the nerve pathways. Some of your nerves, like the ones from each eye, only carry messages to the brain. They are **sensory nerves**.

Other nerves only carry messages from your brain to your muscles. The nerve to the larynx in your neck does this so that you can speak. These are called **motor** nerves.

Some nerves, in your tongue for example, carry messages both ways so your brain can recognize the tastes there and also tell your tongue to move. These are known as mixed nerves.

### What happens where?

The brain's outer layer or cortex looks the same all over. But different areas, or centers, deal with nerve messages going from or to different body parts.

## Control centers

You feel a touch on your skin. But where in your brain do the nerve messages end up?

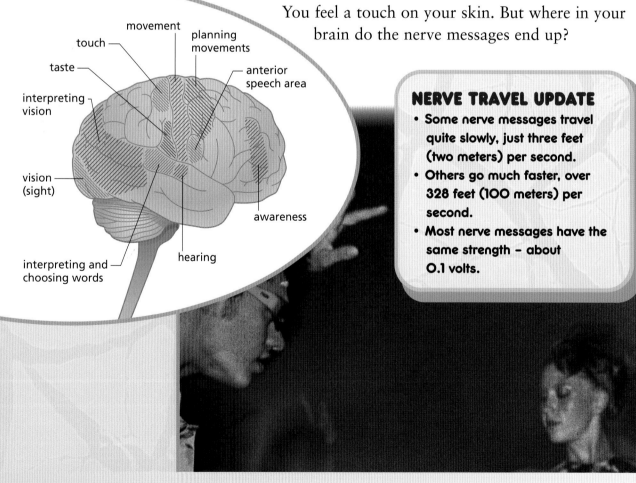

movement
touch
taste
interpreting vision
vision (sight)
interpreting and choosing words
hearing
planning movements
anterior speech area
awareness

### NERVE TRAVEL UPDATE
- Some nerve messages travel quite slowly, just three feet (two meters) per second.
- Others go much faster, over 328 feet (100 meters) per second.
- Most nerve messages have the same strength – about 0.1 volts.

**motor**   causes movements
**sensory nerve**   nerve that carries messages from a sensor or sense organ, such as the eye or skin, to the brain

They go to the touch center, which is a strap-shaped area of **cortex** running over the top of your brain, from one ear to the other. The touch center is where your mind becomes aware of things touching your skin, and works out what they are.

## Making a move

Just in front of the touch center is the **motor center.** This is where you decide to make your movements and get them started.

There are many other centers in the cortex, each with a special job, such as seeing, hearing, tasting, understanding words, and speaking.

## Center problems

Sometimes a head injury affects the way the brain's centers work. For example, a person might suffer damage to the hearing center in the cortex. Then he or she is unable to hear, even though the ears still work normally.

## Seeing stars

A blow to the back of the head may cause a person to see stars. The vision center is at the back area of the brain. A knock to this part of the head may disturb the nerve messages passing through the center, and cause the person to see flashing spots.

◄ Lights, sounds, smells, tastes, and touches are detected by the body's **sense organs.** But it is only when the messages get to the brain that we become aware of them and understand what they mean.

**sense organs**   body parts, such as the nose and ears, used in the senses

# Running on Auto

## Automatic control

The brain stem has its own control centers for heartbeat, breathing, digesting food, altering the amount of blood flowing to different body parts, getting rid of wastes, and many other inner processes.

What have you done so far today? Run for the bus? Eaten breakfast? You probably didn't think of the most important things, like breathing, making your heart beat, and moving food through your intestines. They seem to happen by themselves, automatically without any thought on your part. Yet your brain controls them, too.

brain stem –
midbrain controls
blinking and hearing

cerebrum

pons – some aspects
of breathing

cerebellum

medulla oblongata –
swallowing
breathing
digestion
heartbeat

spinal cord

**brain stem** lowest part of the brain. All signals between the spinal cord and higher parts of the brain pass through. It is also where automatic actions are controlled.

## Two brains in one?

Sometimes it might seem like you have two brains. You are aware of one, your thinking mind. You aren't aware of the other, which works by itself and controls things automatically. But all this happens in the same single brain.

The thinking mind is mainly based in the upper parts of the brain. Automatic control is carried out by the lower parts, mainly the **brain stem**. This is the stalklike part at the base of the brain. Its lower end merges into the top of the body's main nerve, the **spinal cord**.

### Burning up!

Body temperature is controlled by the brain stem. But sometimes, if we fall ill, the control goes wrong. We get too hot, which is called a **fever.** We become sweaty and look red or flushed. We may need cooling with damp towels or a fan, until we feel better.

◄ Playing a musical instrument and singing at the same time is difficult. Imagine if you also had to remember to make your heart beat and your lungs breathe every second. Luckily the brain controls many body processes without you having to think about them.

## Look out!

You are sitting quietly, reading. Suddenly, a big spider crawls across the page. Most people would react at once. Perhaps you would carefully put the book down so you don't harm the spider. Or you may jump up and shout in panic. This shows how your brain can control fast reactions and make your body go from resting still to quick movement in less than a second.

## Autoreactions

Some types of body reactions happen and finish even before you realize they have started. These are called **reflexes.** You probably blink your eyes over 30,000 times every day. Each blink is a reflex that washes away dirt and germs. If your nose gets blocked by dust, the reflex that clears it is sneezing. If you've eaten some bad food, then your stomach gets rid of it by another reflex, vomiting.

## Bundles of reflexes

New babies haven't learned to control their bodies. Their actions are mainly reflexes. They grasp anything within reach. They throw out their arms if you move them too fast or startle them. Gradually as they grow and the nervous system matures, these are replaced by actions performed on purpose.

### TEST YOUR REACTIONS

Ask a friend to hold a ruler at the 12-inch (30-cm) end, so the zero end hangs down. Put your hands on either side of the ruler, level with its lower end. Your friend lets go, and you clap hands together to catch the ruler. The measurement where your hands touch the ruler indicates your reaction speed. Do your reactions get better with practice?

reflex  automatic reaction such as coughing or blinking

## Saved from danger

Reflexes help to keep you safe because they happen so fast. They take place immediately and automatically in your body, under the control of **nerve** circuits in that particular part. Then, quickly, nerve messages pass to your brain, so you become aware of what has happened.

You may be deep in thought doing something else when you touch a sharp point or hot object. Your skin detects this and, before you fully realize what is happening, your reflexes move you away from the danger.

▼ If a fast moving ball comes toward your head unexpectedly, you will automatically close your eyes, twist away, and throw up your hands. These are all reflex reactions to protect your eyes and face. It is almost impossible not to flinch.

## Fast reactions

Reflexes happen very fast, but so do some of your conscious reactions! When sprinters begin a race, their ears hear the starting sound and pass the message to their brains. Then their brains send messages out to their leg muscles. The faster the sprinter's reactions, the better the chance of winning.

# Awake and Asleep

For about one-third of your life, you are asleep. Does your brain switch off at this time? No, it is just as busy as when you are awake. Millions of nerve signals pass through the sleeping brain, as they do in the waking brain. But they are different kinds of signals. The brain-wave lines of the **EEG** machine are different while awake and at sleep. Scientists know a lot about what happens in the brain during sleep. But there's still a great mystery about why we sleep.

## Yawn

Why do we yawn when we are tired, bored, or just waking up? No one is really sure. Maybe we breathe less deeply when we feel tired. Then we get less **oxygen,** which we need to stay alive. A yawn is an extra deep breath that increases the amount of oxygen.

Sleep testing is often ➤ used to try to solve the mysteries of our dreams and sleep patterns.

**Body language**    oxygen    gas that makes up one-fifth of the air we breathe

## Rerunning the day

As you sleep, your body rests and saves energy. It repairs small amounts of normal wear and tear that happen every day. But what is your busy brain doing? Perhaps it goes through the events and memories of the day, like playing a recording. It sorts out the important details. Then it can forget the less important ones and leave memory space for the rest.

## Changing brainwaves

The up-and-down brain waves on the EEG machine indicate being fully awake, daydreaming, feeling tired, and then being fast asleep. In general, the waves become taller and wider as we go from alert to asleep.

*EEG waves show brain activity ...*

*... which varies according to sleep phase.*

23

## How much sleep?

On average, a baby needs about 14 hours of sleep, a ten-year-old needs 10–11 hours, and an adult needs 7–8 hours. But no one is average and we all need slightly different amounts of sleep. If we feel tired and can't concentrate during the day, we're not getting enough sleep at night.

## Zzzzzz

When you go to sleep, you might not be aware of anything until the next morning. But your brain is very busy all night, and in different ways, too.

When you first nod off, you soon go into deep **NREM sleep.** Your muscles are relaxed. Your heartbeat, breathing, and other body processes slow down.

## Flickering eyes

But after an hour or so, your muscles tense and twitch. In particular, your eyes dart back and forth, as though you are looking at an exciting scene, yet your eyelids stay closed. This is called **REM (Rapid Eye Movement) sleep.**

After another 30–60 minutes, you go from REM sleep back to deep sleep (nonREM, or NREM sleep). These changes happen several times, from REM sleep to deep sleep and back again, until it is morning.

## Dreams

Do you dream much? Yes, you probably dream almost every night. But you may not remember your dreams.

People who are awakened from REM sleep nearly always say they have been dreaming. They can usually recall their dreams. But people who wake during deep sleep rarely recall any dreams. Like the puzzle of why we sleep, the reasons why we have deep and REM sleep, and why we dream, are still mostly a mystery.

NREM sleep   period of sleep when the body is very relaxed, the heartbeat and breathing are slow, there are no dreams, and it is difficult to wake up

## Not enough sleep

Lack of sleep brings problems like headaches, poor concentration, loss of memory, clumsy movements, and bad moods. We are more likely to have accidents and suffer illnesses. A good night's sleep is one of our greatest health needs.

▲ Some people fall asleep almost anywhere. This is especially true when we are very young and active through the day, running around, and playing and learning, or if we've stayed up late.

### LIGHT SLEEPER?

Luckily, we don't switch off when we sleep. We still react to changes in our environment, like touches, smells, or sounds. We need this ability in order to protect ourselves. For example, people have been able to smell smoke when asleep, and get out of their home to escape a fire.

**REM** (Rapid Eye Movement) **sleep** period of sleep when the body is less relaxed, the heartbeat and breathing quicken, the eyes flicker, and dreams occur

# Sense-ational!

Are you sensitive? Of course, your body has five main **senses** These are eyes for sight, ears for hearing, nose for smell, tongue for taste, and skin for touch.

Each of these senses detects different types of changes in your surroundings and sends nerve messages to your brain. Your brain takes in all the information from your different senses and decides what to do.

## What a sight!

For most people, sight is the main sense for getting around, carrying out daily tasks, and taking in information. The eye is specialized to change light into millions of nerve messages every second.

## Inside the eye

The eye's pea-sized **lens** bends light like a camera lens to give a clear, sharp view that shines onto the inner lining, the **retina.** This contains millions of cells. When light hits them, they send nerve messages to the brain.

Light passes into the eye ➤ through the eye's clear **cornea,** then through the pupil, into the dark interior of the eyeball.

lens

iris

pupil

eye moving muscle

optic nerve

cornea

aqueous humor

ciliary muscle

retina

choroid

sclera

cornea   clear, curved membrane at the front of the eye

About two-thirds of the information and knowledge in the brain comes in through the eyes when we read words and look at pictures, diagrams, photographs, and what is happening around us.

## Bright eyes

Light shines into your eye through the dark hole or **pupil.** In dim light, your pupils open wide to let in as much light as possible. In bright light they shrink to reduce the amount of light getting in and protect the sensitive cells at the back of your eye.

## Security scan

The colored part of the eye is a ring of muscle called the **iris.** It has a different pattern and color in every person. The iris can be scanned or photographed for security, like fingerprints, to check identity.

Enter name and number: **xxxx xxxxxxx**

A1
B3
C1
D7
E1

SCANNING FOR MATCH

(xrr: 1000223)

SEARCHING DATABASE /
CONFIRMING IDENTITY

Access granted )

## EYE SEE!

- Your eyeball is about 1 inch (2.5 cm) across.
- Six tiny muscles behind the eye make it move to look up, down and to the side.
- The retina has more than 6 million cone cells. These see details and colors, but only work in bright light.
- The retina has more than 120 million cells called rods. These can only see shades of grey, but work well without much light.

**retina** innermost layer of the eye. It receives light rays and sends the information to the brain as nerve signals. The retina makes it possible to see images.

## How you hear

Your ear is shaped to gather sound waves. They travel from outside into a tube, the ear canal. The waves bounce off the round eardrum, which vibrates. Movements pass along three tiny bones to the coil-shaped **cochlea.** Inside this, tiny cells change the vibrations into nerve messages and send these to the brain.

## All ears

Sit still and listen closely. What can you hear? We are hardly ever in a silent place. There are usually sounds of some kind, including people, traffic, wind, rain, birds, and many more.

Your ears pick up these noises, and send **nerve** messages to your brain. But some sounds are just too quiet for our ears. Others are too high and shrill (**ultrasound**) or too low and deep (**infrasound**).

If you have pets like dogs, cats, rabbits, and horses, you've probably noticed they have much better hearing than we do. They prick up their ears at sounds that we can't hear at all.

> We shut our eyes if light is too ➤ bright. We can only shut our ears to protect them from loud noises by putting our hands over them.

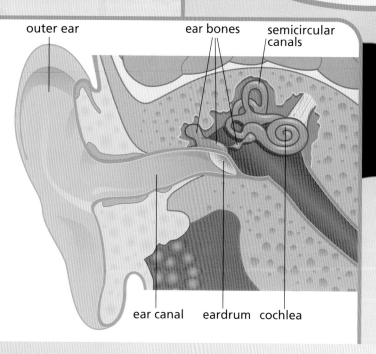

outer ear　　　ear bones　　semicircular canals

ear canal　　eardrum　cochlea

　　cochlea　small, coil-shaped part in the ear lined with hair cells that send sound wave information to the brain as nerve signals

## Over here. No, over there.

Unlike animals, you can't prick up your ears. But like them, you can tell where a sound comes from.

Sounds travel as invisible waves through the air. These move at about 1100 feet (335 meters) per second. If a sound comes from the right, it reaches your right ear about 1/1000th of a second before the left ear hears it. Sounds also lose loudness or volume as they travel. So the sound from the right is louder in your right ear than your left.

Your brain detects the tiny differences in time and loudness between your ears, and works out the direction of a sound. This is called **stereophonic** hearing. For anyone deaf in one ear, this doesn't work.

## WARNING!

Too much loud noise can damage the delicate ear. There are laws for work places about safe sound levels, which are measured in decibels (dB).

160dB
150dB
120dB
100dB
60dB
0dB

quietest sound you can hear
normal conversation
power tools
ears start to hurt
trumpet blown 4 in (10 cm away)
burst eardrums

## Well balanced

The semicircular canals deep inside your ear do not detect sounds. They feel movements and the downward pull of gravity. They send nerve messages to your brain. Your brain combines this information with messages from your eyes, skin, muscles, and joints. This helps you to keep your balance as you move around. Ear infections can make people lose their balance and feel dizzy.

**stereophonic**   able to detect the direction of a sound because of the slight differences in sound waves heard by the right and left ears

## Up your nose!

Your nostrils lead to two thumb-sized spaces inside, the **nasal chambers.** At their tops are two patches, each the size of a thumbnail. They contain 25 million tiny cells with very small hairs sticking from them.

When you breathe in, smelly particles in the air stick to the hairs, and the cells send nerve messages to the brain.

## What's that smell?

What was the last strong smell you remember? Flowers? Last night's dinner? Maybe perfume, the swimming pool, a sweaty locker room, or a cleaning spray?

Smells can bring back strong memories and powerful feelings. This is because nerve messages from your nose go to parts of the brain involved in feelings, emotions, and memories. Messages from other senses don't go directly to these parts.

## Why smells seem to fade

After you detect a strong smell, it seems to fade. But maybe it is still there, and just as strong.

Parts of your brain gradually stop the smell's nerve messages from going into your thoughts. This is because a smell you have already detected becomes less important, and you need to be aware of new smells instead.

## Keeping your mind clear

All of your sensory cells react in the same way. Think about the new sounds of a school or the feel of new shoes. After a while you don't notice them. This is called habituation and it is very helpful. It means your mind and thoughts aren't clogged up with information that is already familiar. Your thinking mind becomes aware only of new or changed sensations.

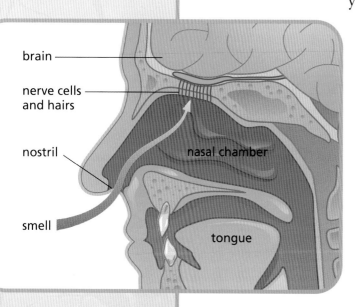

brain

nerve cells and hairs

nostril

nasal chamber

smell

tongue

**nasal chambers**   hollow parts between the nostrils and upper throat, where smells are detected

We hate the smells that come from rotten food, old trash, and animal droppings. This is helpful. It means our senses are warning us to stay away from these smells. Otherwise, we could catch germs and disease.

## Good or bad?

What do you love to smell, and what do you hate? Put these smells in a list, from good to bad. Ask your friends to do the same. Did you all make the same choices?

vinegar

strong cheese

fresh bread

oranges

camp-fire smoke

chocolate sauce

garlic

just-mowed grass

apple pie

## SMELLS LIKE...

Have you ever thought of somebody, or "gone back" to a certain event, because a smell reminded you? For example, smells such as a campfire, or the seashore, may trigger happy memories.

## Terrific tastes

Can you remember the flavors of your food yesterday? Sometimes we rush to eat and hardly taste a thing. If we take more time, we can enjoy food's tastes, its textures, such as crunchy, flaky, lumpy, or creamy, and its temperature. These feelings of texture and temperature come from the sense of touch inside your mouth.

As you are chewing, smells from food pass up the back of your mouth through your nose chamber to your smell sensors. So what you think of as taste is really your senses of taste, smell, and touch all working together.

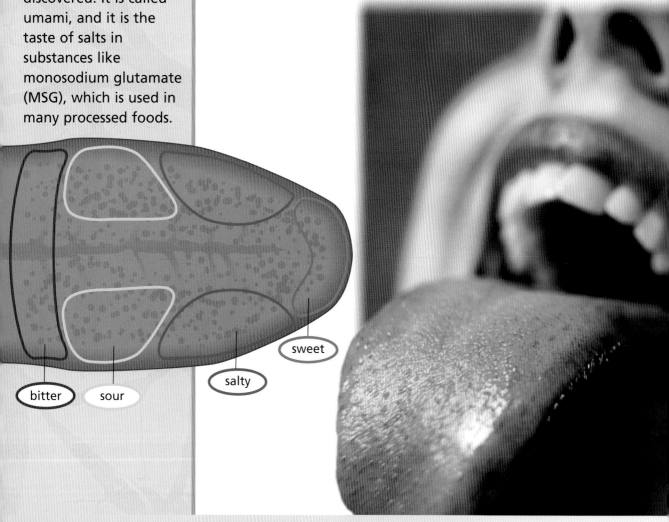

bitter

sour

salty

sweet

## Tongue's tasks

Your tongue doesn't just taste your food. It moves the food around inside your mouth so you can chew it properly. You've seen the tiny bumps all over your tongue, called **papillae.** There are four kinds and three of them contain taste buds.

Your tongue also licks food that dribbles off your lips. And it moves when you talk, so you can speak words clearly. Try saying *hello* without moving your tongue.

### TASTE CHALLENGE

Ask a friend to close their eyes, and with a clean spoon, put a small amount of sugar on the tip of their tongue. Can they tell it is sugar?

After a water mouthwash, try salt on the tongue tip. Can they guess what it is, or do they need to move it to another area of the tongue to recognize the salty taste?

Next, try putting some lemon juice on their tongue. Can they guess what it is?

### Don't be silly, it tastes great!

Taste buds gradually die away over the years. So tastes and flavors seem stronger for young people compared to older people. Also, breathing in fumes or smoke, as you do if you smoke cigarettes, damages your taste buds, and makes flavors dull.

◀ You taste with your tongue's 10,000 **taste buds,** beside and between the papillae. Taste buds are far too small to see, shaped like tiny oranges made of microscopic cells, with hairs sticking out. Taste particles in food stick to the hairs and the cells send nerve messages to the brain.

**taste buds**   cone-shaped groups of cells on the tongue that detect tastes

## Getting in touch

The sense based in your skin is called touch. But it detects far more than being touched.

Imagine your eyes are closed and you have to guess what an object is by touch alone. You feel very carefully for its shape and size. Is its surface smooth or lumpy, slippery, or rough? Are there any edges or ridges? You press to see if the object is hard or soft. You can also detect if it is warm or cold and perhaps wet or dry.

Your skin senses these many different features. So touch is not as simple as it seems.

### Inside skin

Touch is detected by sensory receptors just under the skin's surface layer. They send nerve messages to the brain. Disk-shaped sensors near the surface feel light touch. Blob-shaped ones lower down sense pressure. Branched ones, like tiny trees, detect pain.

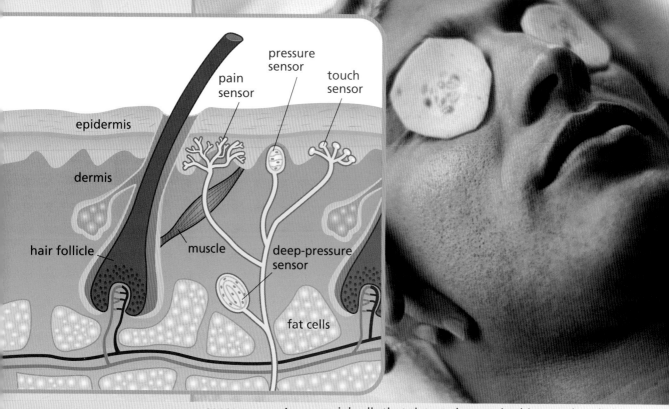

epidermis

dermis

hair follicle

muscle

pain sensor

pressure sensor

touch sensor

deep-pressure sensor

fat cells

**sensory receptors** special cells that detect changes in things such as light, texture, and temperature. This information is communicated to sensory neurons that take the information to the brain.

## Fingertips and lips

If you try the test, you would probably use your fingers. These are very sensitive for touch. Your eyelids, lips and tongue are also very sensitive.

All these areas have lots of **sensory receptors** that detect touch. One fingertip has more than 3,000 receptors packed close together. Other areas of skin, like the lower back and front thigh, have fewer receptors, so they are less touch-sensitive.

## Ouch!

Skin has another sense that we don't like—pain. But we need pain. It warns if our skin and the body underneath are getting damaged. Then we can take care to prevent any more harm and keep protected.

### DID YOU KNOW?

Hairs cannot feel touch because they are dead. (Otherwise a haircut would be very painful.) However, each hair has sensors around its base in the skin. These sense the hair being pulled or moved. Sometimes when you feel something, nothing actually contacts your skin. You are feeling your tiny body hairs being moved.

◀Touch affects our mood. Some kinds can be very soothing, like a gentle massage or stroking. Other touches are strange, funny, or scary.

## Itching an d scratching

Why does skin feel an itch? It might be a tiny insect walking or a mosquito biting. It could be one of your skin's tiny hairs, bent over and rubbing the surface. It may be bits of dust from the air setting off the sensors. A quick scratch usually works, but an itch caused by an illness, such as a rash, may need to be seen by the doctor.

# Chemical Control

Your brain controls most body parts by sending messages along **nerves**. But there is another control system, too. This is based not on nerve messages, but natural body chemicals called **hormones** produced by the endocrine system.

Your mind is not aware of how hormones are made or work. But you often feel their effects. When you are very frightened, thirsty, or worried, hormones are involved. They also control how the body grows and how it repairs damage.

In general, hormones are in charge of slow processes that take from hours to weeks and years, such as growing. Nerves control faster processes that happen in seconds or minutes, such as movement.

## Hormone glands

Some hormone glands make just one hormone. Others produce several. A few body parts make hormones in addition to their main jobs. These include the heart and stomach.

**The body parts that make hormones**

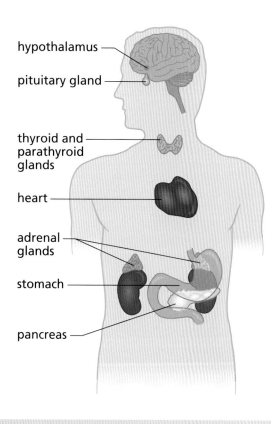

- hypothalamus
- pituitary gland
- thyroid and parathyroid glands
- heart
- adrenal glands
- stomach
- pancreas

target organs  body parts affected by a certain hormone. The heart is one of epinephrine's target organs.

## Where are hormones made?

There are dozens of hormones, each affecting different body processes. They are made in about ten **endocrine glands**. Your blood stream carries the hormones from these glands all around your body. As they reach certain body organs, they affect how those parts work.

In general, a larger amount of hormone makes the organ work faster. The brain, nerves, and hormones keep all your body parts working together.

### HORMONES ON TARGET

- Each hormone controls certain body parts, called its target organs.
- Certain hormones have just a few target organs, like the heart or stomach.
- Other hormones affect almost every cell. The whole body is their target.

## Nerves and stress

When we feel nervous, anxious or worried, this is partly the result of more hormones in the blood. These stress hormones, including cortisol and epinephrine, put us on edge. These hormones act quickly.

◄ Hormones control water in the body. If there is too much, they make the extra water pass into urine. If there is not enough water, hormones reduce the amount of urine, and your brain tells you that you are thirsty.

## Little yet big

Sometimes small things can be very important. This is true of your **pituitary.** It is behind your eyes, at the lower front of your brain, and only the size of a pea. Yet it makes more than ten **hormones.** Most of these control how other hormone glands work. So your pituitary is the boss of your whole endocrine system.

## Double control

However, your pituitary does not work by itself. It is joined by a narrow stalk to the brain part above it called the **hypothalamus.** The hypothalamus is involved in powerful feelings and emotions like anger, fear, and joy.

Nerve signals and chemical substances pass from the hypothalamus along the stalk to the pituitary and tell it when to set free its hormones. This is how your body's nervous and endocrine systems are linked.

### Twin tasks

The **pancreas,** behind the stomach, has two main jobs. One is to make powerful chemicals that digest food in the intestines. The other is making two hormones, insulin and glucagon. These control the glucose in the blood, your main source of energy.

The pituitary (seen from the ➤ front in this brain scan) is linked to the brain by a thin strip or stalk. Messages pass along this as **nerve signals** and hormonelike chemicals, so here the nerve system and hormone system work together.

hypothalamus

brain

stalk of pituitary

pituitary

pancreas    body organ that makes chemicals for digestion and hormones to control the level of glucose in the blood

## In the neck

The **thyroid** gland in your neck makes hormones to control how fast your body's millions of cells work. If the thyroid isn't working right, the whole body slows down and feels very tired, or speeds up and works too fast. Usually these problems can be treated with medicines.

◄ People with diabetes may need regular injections and also have to be be careful about what they eat.

**pituitary**   pea-sized gland at base of the brain that makes many hormones
**thyroid**   H-shaped gland at the base of the neck that makes hormones important for growth and development

## Run for it!

BOO! Has something frightened you lately?

When you are surprised or afraid, do you feel your heart thumping and butterflies in your stomach? Your skin gets sweaty and your muscles tense, ready for fast movement. These changes are partly the result of nerve messages and partly due to the hormone called **epinephrine**.

## Through the pain barrier

Some athletes carry on even when they are exhausted or injured. They don't seem to notice the hardship and pain. This is due to the effects of epinephrine and other hormones. Their nerves may tell them to stop because of pain, but their hormones and willpower say keep going.

Some people like the ➤ excitement of being scared, especially when they know they are really safe. These feeling are brought on by nerves and also by the hormone epinephrine.

adrenals   two glands, one on top of each kidney, that make several hormones including epinephrine

## A big buzz

Epinephrine is made in your **adrenals,** two hormone glands on top of your kidneys. Epinephrine works with your brain and nerves to get your body ready for action. For example, it changes the way blood flows around your body. Less blood flows to your skin and to your stomach and guts, and more blood rushes to the muscles you would use to run away!

This is why, when you are scared, your skin turns pale, and you feel a tightening or fluttering inside your stomach.

## Water, energy, stress, repair

The adrenals make other hormones as well as epinephrine. These other hormones affect growth, alter the amount of water in urine, help to control blood sugar for energy, help the body cope with stress, and repair everyday wear-and-tear.

The affects of epinephrine and nerves cause the fight-or-flight reaction. Your body makes itself ready to stay and battle the danger or run away. Here are the symptoms:

- Heart beats faster
- Lungs breathe faster and deeper
- More blood flows to muscles
- Less blood flows to other body parts (skin, intestines)
- Pupils of eyes open wide
- Skin sweats
- Tiny hairs in skin stand on end, making goosebumps
- Senses become extra-alert
- Brain prepares to make fast decisions

## Oh, grow up!

You can snap your fingers in a second. Fast actions like this are usually controlled by **nerves.** But growing from a baby to an adult takes about 20 years. Slow processes are controlled by **hormones.** The main hormone affecting growth is called growth hormone. It comes from the chief hormone gland, the **pituitary** under the brain.

## Up and up

Our full grown body height, when we are adults, is controlled mainly by the **genes** we inherit from our parents. But how fast we grow to this adult height is partly due to growth hormone.

## Changing bones

Growing does not just mean getting bigger. Inside the body, as the bones of the skeleton grow, they change shape and become harder. This is another long, slow process controlled mainly by hormones.

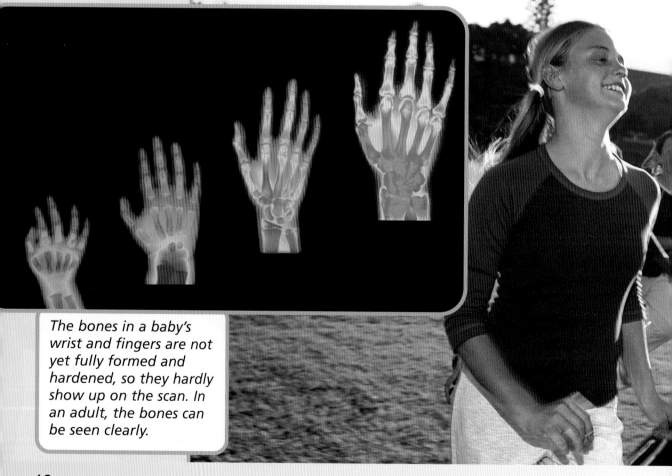

*The bones in a baby's wrist and fingers are not yet fully formed and hardened, so they hardly show up on the scan. In an adult, the bones can be seen clearly.*

42    **Body language**    **genes** chemical instructions for how the body grows, develops, and works

Some people naturally have slightly more of it. So they grow faster and reach their adult height younger, compared to those with slightly less growth hormone. This is all part of the normal, natural differences between people.

## Too much, too little

In very rare cases, the pituitary makes too much growth hormone by mistake. Then the body grows very fast. Or the pituitary makes too little, and the body stays small. Luckily these problems can be treated by medicines.

▼ These young people are all about the same age. But they are different heights, partly due to the effects of growth hormone.

### Yes, master

The human brain does not work as fast or have as much memory as some computers. Also, the body's control system of **nerves** and hormones is not always perfect. But imagine a robot with a supercomputer brain and a perfect machinelike body. It would always be right and never go wrong. It could soon become very boring!

# Find Out More

## Books
Hains, Bryan C. *Brain Disorders*. New York: Chelsea House Publishers, 2006

Hayhurst, Chris. *The Brain and Spinal Cord: Learning How We Think, Feel and Move*. New York: Rosen Publishing, 2000

Parker, Steve. *The Brain and Nervous System*. Chicago: Raintree, 2004

## World Wide Web
If you want to find out more about muscles and bones, you can search the Internet using keywords like these:

● "eye sight"   ● eardrum + decibels   ● fight or flight

You can also find your own keywords by using headings or words from this book. Use the search tips below to help you find the most useful websites.

### Where to search

#### Search engine
A search engine looks through millions of Web site pages. It lists all the sites that match the words in the search box. It can give thousands of links, but you will find the best matches are at the top of the list, on the first page. Try **google.com**

#### Search directory
A search directory is like a library of Web sites that has been sorted by a person instead of a computer. You can search by keyword or subject and browse through the different sites like you look through books on a library shelf. A good example is **yahooligans.com**

### Search tips
There are billions of pages on the Internet. It can be difficult to find exactly what you are looking for. These tips will help you find useful Web sites more quickly:

● Know what you want to find out about.
● Use two to six keywords in a search, putting the most important words first.
● Be precise—only use names of people, places, or things.
● If you want to find words that go together, put quote marks around them, for example, "stomach acid."
● Use the advanced section of your search engine.
● Use the + sign between keywords to link them.

# Glossary

**adrenals** two glands, one on top of each kidney, that make several hormones including epinephrine

**axons** parts of a nerve cell that take messages from the main cell body to other nerve cells

**brain stem** lowest part of the brain. All signals between the spinal cord and the higher parts of the brain pass through it. It is also where automatic actions are controlled.

**cells** microscopic building blocks that make up all body parts

**cerebellum** part at the rear of the brain that controls muscle actions

**cerebral cortex** thin gray layer covering the cerebrum (main upper part of the brain). It is involved in thinking, memory, experiencing the surroundings through the senses, planning movements, and many other mental activities.

**cerebral hemispheres** two halves of the cerebrum, the largest part of the brain

**cerebrum** upper portion of the brain with white matter inside and a surface layer of gray matter. It receives information from the senses.

**cochlea** small, coil-shaped part in the ear lined with hair cells that send sound wave information to the brain as nerve signals

**cornea** clear, curved membrane at the front of the eye

**CSF** cerebrospinal fluid. It cushions the brain and the spinal cord.

**dendrites** parts of a nerve cell that take messages from nerve cells to the main cell body

**EEG (electroencephalogram)** records electrical activity in the brain

**endocrine glands** tissue that makes chemicals

**epinephrine** hormone that gets the body ready for quick action if needed. It is produced during exercise and when the body experiences fear and excitement.

**fever** higher than normal body temperature, when the person may feel hot and sweaty, or may shiver

**genes** chemical instructions for how the body grows, develops, and works

**glucagon** hormone made by the pancreas. It raises the level of glucose in the blood.

**glucose** sugar obtained from the breakdown of carbohydrates in food. It is the body's main source of energy.

**hippocampus** part of the brain that is important for memory

**hormones** chemical substances made by glands that help the body carry out various processes

**hypothalamus** small part of the brain that deals with emotions and automatic processes, such as maintaining body temperature

**infrasound** sounds which are too low in pitch for a person to hear

**insulin** hormone made by the pancreas. It lowers the level of glucose in the blood.

**iris**  ring of muscle at the front of the eye, between the white part and the pupil, that gives the eye its color

**lens**  thin layer behind the pupil that bends or focuses light into the inside of the eyeball to form images

**meninges**  three thin layers around the brain and spinal cord that protect and nourish them. They are called the dura mater, arachnoid, and pia mater.

**motor**  causes movements

**motor center**  strap-shaped region on brain's cerebral cortex that is involved in control of muscle movements

**nasal chambers**  hollow parts between the nostrils and the upper throat, where smells are detected

**nerve cell**  cell specialized to receive, process, and send on nerve messages, in the form of tiny pulses of electricity

**nerves**  stringlike tissue that carries messages around the body as tiny pulses of electricity

**NREM (non-REM) sleep**  period of sleep when the body is very relaxed, the heartbeat and breathing are slow, there are no dreams, and it is difficult to wake up

**oxygen**  gas that makes up one-fifth of the air we breathe

**papillae**  small lumps in the dermis. One type can be seen on the surface of the tongue.

**pancreas**  organ that makes chemicals for digestion and hormones to control the level of glucose in the blood

**pituitary**  pea-sized gland just below the brain that makes many hormones

**pupil**  hole in the middle of the eye though which light enters

**reflex**  automatic reaction such as coughing or blinking

**REM (Rapid Eye Movement) sleep**  period of sleep when the body is less relaxed, the heartbeat and breathing quicken, the eyes flicker, and dreams occur

**retina**  innermost layer of the eye. It receives light rays and sends the information to the brain as nerve signals. The retina makes it possible to see images.

**sciatic nerve**  nerve that runs from the pelvis down the back of each leg to the foot

**sense organs**  body parts, such as the nose and ears, used in the senses

**senses**  the ability of the body to detect something such as light, temperature or the level of a certain substance inside itself, and send messages to the brain

**sensor**  part that detects something, like light, sound, or the amount of a certain chemical and sends messages to the brain

**sensory nerve**  nerve that carries messages from a sensor or sense organ, such as the eye or skin, to the brain

**sensory receptors** special cells that detect changes in things such as light, texture, and temperature. This information is communicated to sensory neurons that take the information to the brain.

**skull** main bone in the head, which is really more than 20 bones joined together

**spinal cord** main nerve linking the brain to the rest of the body

**stereophonic** able to detect the direction of a sound because of the slight differences in sound waves heard by the left and right ears

**target organs** body parts affected by a certain hormone. The heart is one of epinephrine's target organs.

**taste buds** cone-shaped groups of cells on the tongue that detect tastes

**thalamus** two walnut-sized lumps of nerve tissue above the brain stem. It takes in information from the sense organs.

**thyroid** H-shaped gland at the base of the neck that makes hormones important for growth and development

**ultrasound** sounds which are too high for a person to hear

**ventricles** chambers or spaces inside a body part, such as the four ventricles inside the brain, which are filled with cerebrospinal fluid

# Index